Silas Wood, William Smith Pelletreau

Silas Wood's Sketch of the Town of Huntington, L. I.

From its First Settlement to the End of the American Revolution

Silas Wood, William Smith Pelletreau

Silas Wood's Sketch of the Town of Huntington, L. I.
From its First Settlement to the End of the American Revolution

ISBN/EAN: 9783337230067

Printed in Europe, USA, Canada, Australia, Japan

Cover: Foto ©ninafisch / pixelio.de

More available books at **www.hansebooks.com**

SILAS WOOD'S SKETCH OF THE TOWN OF HUNTINGTON, L. I.

FROM ITS FIRST SETTLEMENT TO THE END OF THE AMERICAN REVOLUTION.

EDITED WITH GENEALOGICAL AND
HISTORICAL NOTES

BY

WILLIAM S. PELLETREAU, A. M.

NEW YORK:
FRANCIS P. HARPER.
1898.

TO

RICHARD H. HANDLEY, ESQ.,

of Smithtown, Long Island, as a very slight token of
respect, and acknowledgment of many favors
and much assistance in the work of
collecting and preserving history,
this work is respectfully
dedicated.

INTRODUCTION.

Among the earliest settlers on Long Island was Jonas Wood, who came from Halifax, England, and was among the first residents of Hempstead in 1644. He removed to Southampton about 1649 and became the owner of land in the right of " his father-in-law, Mr. Sticklin, of Hempstead." * From Southampton he removed to Huntington, about 1655, and was one of the original purchasers of Copiage and the five necks east, in 1657. Tradition states that he was drowned in Peconic River, between the 20th of April and the 18th of May, 1660.

Joshua Wood, one of his descendants, was born October 12, 1716, and died September 6, 1779, aged 63. He married Ruth Wood, who was born May 26, 1724, and died August 29, 1807, in her 84th year. Their children were Samuel, Selah and Silas. Of these children, the youngest, Silas Wood, who has left a lasting fame as the Historian of Long Island, was born at West Hills, in the town of Huntington, September 14, 1769. At the early age of 16 he entered Princeton College, pursued a full classical course, and graduated from that institution with high honors. In 1795, he was elected Member of Assembly, where he

* See Vol. 1, Printed Records of Southampton, page 47.

served for four years, and introduced the first General Highway Act, which with a few changes has remained in force till the present time.

What was known as the " Great West " at that time meant the western part of the State of New York and the " Ohio region." Mr. Wood became the owner of a large tract in Johnstown, and spent several years in establishing a settlement. In 1802, he married Catharine Huyck, a descendant of one of the Dutch families who settled in the Mohawk valley. She died suddenly while they were on a journey through what was then a wilderness, now Montgomery County, N. Y. Shortly after that he began the study of law, and was admitted to practice in the Supreme Court of that State, February 15, 1810. On March 2nd of the same year, he was appointed Master in Chancery, and in May, 1813, became Solicitor in Chancery. In November, 1817, he was elected Member of Congress, taking his seat March 4, 1819. In this high position he served five terms, a period of ten years. During the whole of his Congressional career he was an earnest opponent of the extension of slavery and a strong supporter of a protective tariff, and never failed to advance the idea that a country like our own should be self-supporting and entirely independent of most of the manufactured products of foreign nations.

From 1818 to 1821, he was District Attorney for Suffolk County, and for a long term of years he was the recognized leader of the Suffolk County Bar.

His "Sketch of the Early Settlements of Long Island," which has made his name famous, was the work of his leisure time for many years. He lived before the days of railroads, and his journeys in pursuit of information were made in a plain box wagon "as plain as himself." In this humble vehicle he traveled throughout the Island visiting the clerks' offices of every town and county. This "Sketch" was first printed in 1824, and was a small volume of 66 pages. A second edition, containing 112 pages, was published in 1826. A third edition, of 183 pages, appeared in 1828. This last edition was printed for the sole purpose of doing honor to the memory of Gen. Nathaniel Woodhull. The first edition of this work was limited to 250 copies, while of the second and third only 100 copies were printed, and it is not strange that copies are now scarce and command a high price. A fine reprint of the work, with a brilliantly written life of its distinguished author by his friend and admirer, Alden J. Spooner, Esq., was issued in 1865.

The "Sketch of the Geography of the Town of Huntington," which is here reprinted, was prepared while the author was in Congress. Of this little work only a limited edition was printed, and a large portion of that was destroyed by a fire that consumed the house of his neighbor, Moses Rolph, and copies of the original pamphlet are exceedingly rare.

In the spring of 1830, Silas Wood withdrew entirely from the world of politics and business, of which he had for many years been so distinguished a part. To make his separation more complete he sold his law library, ceased to take the newspapers, and devoted the remainder of his years to religious contemplation. At the age of 63 he joined the Presbyterian Church. At the time of his death his library consisted entirely of a small number of religious books, which he left to the Presbyterian Church, at Sweet Hollow, near Huntington.

In 1829, he married Elizabeth, daughter of Josiah Smith, of Long Swamp, Huntington. He left no descendants to inherit his fortune or his fame. He died at peace with God and mankind March 2, 1847, in the 78th year of his age. His remains were buried in the Old Hill burying ground, adjoining the Presbyterian Parsonage in Huntington, and one of the plainest of plain tombstones marks his last resting place.

He was farsighted as a statesman, able and convincing as a lawyer, careful and painstaking as a historian, and left behind him a reputation for honor and uprightness that no one could assail.

WILLIAM S. PELLETREAU.

SOUTHAMPTON, L. I., July 12, 1898.

A SKETCH

OF

THE GEOGRAPHY

OF THE

Town of Huntington,

WITH A

BRIEF HISTORY

OF ITS

FIRST SETTLEMENT AND POLITICAL CONDITION

TO THE END OF

THE REVOLUTION.

BY SILAS WOOD.

WASHINGTON :

PRINTED BY DAVIS & FORCE, (FRANKLIN'S HEAD, PENNSYLVANIA AVE.)

1824.

A SKETCH

OF

THE GEOGRAPHY,

OF THE

TOWN OF HUNTINGTON.

———

SITUATION AND EXTENT.

Huntington is the most westerly town in Suffolk county — it comprises a section of the island, extending from the sound to the South-Bay, in its widest part. The principal village lies about 40 miles north easterly from New-York, in 40 deg. 52 min. north latitude, and 73 deg. of longitude, west of Greenwich.

It is bounded on the north by the sound, on the east, by a line running from Fresh Pond to the north-west angle of Winnacomac Patent, and from thence to the creek east of Sunquam's neck; then down said creek to the South-Bay, and from thence south to the ocean. On the south by the ocean, on the west by Cold Spring Harbour, and by a line running from the head of the said harbour, to a creek west of West Neck; then down the said creek to the South-Bay, and from thence running southerly to a monument on the beach, fixed by commissioners appointed by law in 1797.

It extends about 10 miles on the sound, and 6 miles on the South-Bay, and 20 from north to south, and contains nearly 160 square miles.

In 1691, Horse Neck,[1] which lies within the bounds of Huntington Patent, was annexed to Queen's county, by an act of the legislature, and has remained so ever since.

POPULATION.[6]

By the census of 1820, the town of Huntington contained 4935 inhabitants of the following description:

White Males.		White Females.	
Under 10 years, -	728	Ditto. - -	645
Between 10 & 16,	- 344	do. -	- 320
do. 16 & 26,	428	do. -	- 404
do. 26 & 45,	- 464	do. -	- 492
Upwards of 45, -	382	do. -	- 395
	2346		2256

Male Slaves.		Female Slaves.	
Under 14, - -	- 9	do. -	- 10
Between 14 & 26,	- 19	do. -	- 11
do. 26 & 45,	- 5	do. -	- 7
Upwards of 45,	- 1	do. -	- 2
	34		30

Free Coloured Males.		Free Coloured Females.	
Under 14, -	- 40	do. -	- 38
Between 14 & 26,	- 12	do. -	- 44
do. 26 & 45,	22	do. -	- 25
Upwards of 45, -	14	do. -	- 14
	88		121

2

All other persons—60

White Males, -	- 2846	Employed in Agricul-	
White Females,	2256	ture, - - -	1069
Male Slaves, -	- 34	Employed in Trade,	33
Female Slaves,	30	do. as Tradesmen,	261
Free coloured Males,	88		
Free coloured Fe-			1363
males, - - -	121		
Other persons, -	60		

Total, - - 4935

COMPARATIVE POPULATION.

1820.

East Hampton, -	1646
South Hampton,	4229
Shelter-Island, -	389
Brook-Haven,	5218
Islip, - - -	1156
Huntington, -	4935
Smith Town, -	1874
River Head, -	1857
South Old, - -	2968

Suffolk, - -	24272
Queens, -	21519
Kings, - -	11187
	56978

Employment of Males over 16.

	Agricul.	Com.	Manuf.
Suffolk,	4642	342	1093
Queens,	4130	102	1119
Kings,	840	81	713
	9612	525	2931

Males over 16, 14180
Employed in A. C. M., 13068

Unemployed, 1112

	Males.	Females.
	11761	11250
	9643	9040
	5096	4514
	26500	24804 as 13 to 12

3

Proportion of Population of Long-Island to the State of New-York.

	Long-Island.	State.
1731,	- - 17820	- - 50,291 as 1 to 3
1771,	- - 27731	- - 163,338 as 1 to 6
1786,	- - 30863	- - 238,896 as 1 to 7
1790,	- - 36949	- - 340,120 as 1 to 9
1800,	- - 42167	- - 586,141 as 1 to 14
1810,	- - 48752	- - 959,049 as 1 to 19
1820,	- - 56978	- 1,372,812 as 1 to 24

Proportion of Population of New-York to the United States.

	New-York.	United States.
1790,	- 340,120	- - 3,950,000 as 1 to 11
1800,	- - 586,050	- - 5,305,666 as 1 to 9
1810,	- 959,049	- - 7,230,514 as 1 to 7
1820,	- 1,372,812	- - 9,654,415 as 1 to 7

Of the number of taxables in the Town, and the valuation of their real and personal property at different periods.

1687 taxables,	-	84	-	valuation, $	15,088 68
1787 do.	-	458	-	do.	326,352 52
1819 do.	-	648	-	do.	1,253,850 00
1823 do.	-	729	-	do.	811,480 00

Comparative valuation of the several towns in Suffolk.

	Valuat'n. 1804.	Tax.	Valuat'n. 1812.	Tax.	Valuat'n. 1818.	Tax.	Valuat'n. 1823.	Tax.
East Hampton,	315900	78 97	308200	115 57	657900	109 65	464060	154 72
Southampton,	607380	151 85	620490	232 63	1357750	226 29	960305	320 10
Shelter-Island,	77040	19 26	81735	30 54	141490	23 58	105640	35 21
South Old,	407170	101 79	399100	149 66	651600	108 60	534920	178 30
River-Head,	238490	59 62	232891	87 33	388066	64 68	267380	89 12
Brook-Haven,	765910	191 48	768050	288 01	1369580	228 26	969500	323 16
Smith-Town,	418320	104 58	375464	140 79	426675	71 11	320078	106 69
Huntington,	702030	175 51	739720	277 39	1253850	208 98	811480	270 49
Islip,	213400	53 35	219730	82 39	373370	62 23	279349	93 11
	3745640	936 41	3745380	1404 46	6620281	1103 38	4712712	1570 90

Of the several Counties on the Island in 1821.

Kings, $ 3,513,164
Queens,   5,876,775
Suffolk,   4,889,474
───────── Whole State.

$14,279,413—241,283,532 as 1 to 16.

Proportion of the valuation of the County of Suffolk to the State.

	COUNTY.	STATE.
1815	$ 6,834,906	$ 293,882,224 as 1 to 43.
1817	6,676,267	315,370,836 as 1 to 47.
1819	5,327,392	281,068,280 as 1 to 52.
1820	5,267,141	256,605,300 as 1 to 48.
1821	4,889,474	241,283,532 as 1 to 49.

CLIMATE.

The insular situation of this town renders it more temperate than places in the same parallel of latitude, at a distance from the sea. In the summer it is regularly fanned by a sea breeze, which generally rises afternoon, but sometimes before, and extends more or less across the Island, according to the strength and continuance of the wind. In the winter the predominant winds are from the west and southwest. The thermometer seldom sinks below zero in winter, and seldom rises higher than 90 degrees in summer. The mean temperature of the year is about 51 degrees,* and the weather is clear three-fifths of the year.

*The mean temperature of Italy 30 years before the birth of Christ, was about 51—in the year 1783, it was 68. The mean temperature of the different places in Europe is about 10 degs. higher than the corresponding latitudes in the United States, and this is found, by experiment, to be about the difference of the temperature of the earth in cleared and uncleared land.

5

White frost happens when the thermometer is
at 49 degs.
And black do. . . . . at 39 degs.
Peach trees bloom the last of April.
Apple trees bloom the 10th of May.
The white oak begins to leave 20th of May.
The dog wood blossoms 1st of June.
Pasture is fit for horses the 20th of May, and con-
tinues till the 20th of November.
Cattle need some kind of provender for six months
in the year.

The following are the results of a series of observa-
tions made in Huntington for 455 days, commencing
the 1st September, 1821.

Greatest Heat.	*Greatest Cold.*
1822, July 4—94	1822, January 5—5 below zero.
do. 20—94	do. 14—4 do.
	do. 24—at zero.
September 3—94	do. 25—2 below.

The mean temperature of the several months in the
year from the 1st September, 1821 to 1st September,
1822.

			Winds.		
September,	-	67 degrees.			
October,	-	54 do.	North,	-	20
November,	-	43 do.	Northwest,	-	41
December,	-	32 do.	Northeast,	-	52
January,	-	25 do.	East,	-	59
February,	-	30 do.	Southeast,	-	21
March,	-	41 do.	South,	-	25

April,	- 48 degrees.
May,	- 61 do.
June,	- 69 do.
July,	- 75 do.
August,	- 72 do.

The mean of the
year, - - 51

Temperature of
deep wells and
springs, - - 51

Winds.

Southwest,	- 120
West,	- 117
	———
	455

Weather.

Clear,	- 270
Cloudy,	- 113
Rainy,	- 51
Snowy,	- 21
	———
	455*

SURFACE OF THE COUNTRY.

The surface of this town along the sound, and for two or three miles from it, is rough and uneven, and in some places stony—it then becomes level, and continues so from 2 to 4 miles in different places, when there are three separate short ridges or groups of hills; to wit, the west hills, the hilly land around the long swamp and Dix hills—these are irregular, and extend two or three miles in length, and nearly the same in breadth. South westerly of Dix hills, after a small interval of level land, there is another tract of elevated

*Note—The mean temperature at the City of Washington, was as follows:

September	72.10	March.	44
October	57.11	April	52.30
November	42.21	May	65.30
December	32.30	June	69.40
January	24.45	July	73.20
February	33	August	76

And the mean temperature of the year 53.35.

7

land rising in the midst of the plain land, and extends about three miles east and west, and about two miles north and south, called the half-way hollow hills.

From these different hills, there is a gentle descent to the South-Bay, but it is so gradual and imperceptible as not to be distinguished from a perfect plain—the rise from the South-Bay to the high land, near the sound, not being supposed to exceed 10 feet in a mile.

The South-Bay is bordered with salt and sedge meadows about one mile deep; north of these meadows, there is a strip of oak-timber from one to two miles wide; from this strip of timber, which is called the south woods, north to the hills and high lands, a distance of from 5 to 10 miles; in different places, *the whole country is a barren pitch-pine and shrub oak plain.*

SOIL.

The soil on the neck's on the sound is usually good, and is the best land in the town—for nearly 10 miles from the sound, the soil is tolerably good; and with manure, is capable of being rendered very productive —it then becomes more sandy. The soil on the hills and high land is usually the best and most productive.

The pine plain is a bed of sand, with intervals of a thin covering of sandy loam, and is uninhabited, except near the creeks that head there.

The tract of land which lies between the plains and the salt meadows, is the only land that is cultivated on the south side—the soil is generally a very sandy loam; it is a thin but kind soil, and many of the proprietors, by the aid of the grass produced by the meadows and islands in the South Bay, and the sea weed that drifts on the shores, have rendered their farms quite productive, especially in grain; but the soil is so porous, that the same process must be continually renewed to keep them so.

The soil of every part of the town is more or less mixed with sand, and is deficient in moisture—it is very liable to suffer by drought, and is much better adapted to grain than grass.

The south meadows and the islands in the South-Bay produce an abundance of salt and sedge grass, and are admirably well calculated to remedy the defects of the soil by furnishing the inhabitants with a substitute for English hay, for the support of their stock.

AGRICULTURE.

The inhabitants of this town have, within twenty years, generally begun to improve their farms by manure, and in some instances they have brought them into a high state of cultivation. Those who live on the north and south sides of the Island, possess more advantages with regard to the means of procuring manure, and have availed themselves of their situation. The land on the south side has improved more in value within 20 years than any other part of the town: but many farms on the north side and in the interior of the town have greatly increased in value, and the whole town has been rendered much more productive both in grain and grass than it formerly was. The people, generally, have become much more careful to increase the quantity of their barn yard and other manure, than they formerly were. Those who are able, usually procure leeched ashes and other lighter manures in addition to their own stock. Experience has proved that ashes are the most productive and permanent manure that can be employed in this town. The importation of this article has become a regular business, and forms the largest item in the trade of the town.

WATER.

The high land near the sound and the ridges of hilly land, abound with ponds of standing water; there are few farms without one or more of them, and many of them are left unenclosed for public watering places. Springs abound near the harbours on the north side, and near the creeks on the south side; and there are some excellent Springs at the West Hills and half-way Hollow Hills. The ponds on the high lands supply the beasts—water for domestic use is derived from wells, but on the level land the water is obtained from wells for both purposes. Those on the hilly lands are shallow, but on the level land are deeper, and near the sound very deep, frequently as low as the level of high-water mark.

HARBOURS, BAYS AND CREEKS.

There are several harbours on the sound within the limits of the town—these are Cold Spring Harbour, Lloyd's Harbour, Huntington Harbour, and Great and Little Cow Harbour. The tide rises and falls on an average of about 7 feet in these harbours, and they are navigable for vessels drawing 8 or 10 feet of water. The large bay formed by Eaton's and Lloyd's Neck's, affords water sufficient for vessels of large size, and was a station for some of the ships belonging to the British fleet, during the Revolutionary war. The streams that fall into these harbours, and the heads of the harbours, by means of dams thrown across them, afford accommodations for mills and other water works.

The South-Bay lies between the meadows and the beach, and is about 4 miles wide; it is separated from the ocean by the beach, which is a body of pure fine sand, about a quarter of a mile wide, and reaches from Rockway to South Hampton, nearly 80 miles in extent. There are several inlets or openings in the beach, which form communications between the ocean and the bay, through which vessels pass from one to the other—these inlets are all in the towns of Islip, Oysterbay and Hempstead.

The Fire Island inlet, which is the principal one, is in Islip, a few miles east of Huntington line.

The tide rises and falls in the bay near the inlets about 2 feet, and lessens as the distance from the inlets increases, at Moriches—the rise and fall are scarcely perceptible.

The bay is shallow, but the channels that intersect and traverse it admit of vessels that draw 4 or 5 feet water, and it is navigable for flat bottomed vessels through its whole extent.

The bay is gradually diminishing in width by the sand blown from the beach, which, in the memory of persons now living, has formed large tracts of meadow on the north side of it—it is also becoming more shallow by means of the sand blown from the beach, and forced into it from the sea, by the tide. The meadows are seldom overflowed as they formerly were, and are less productive on that account, and the navigation of the bay is becoming more difficult. During the revolutionary war, privateers of considerable size entered the Fire Island Inlet, which at this time will hardly admit vessels drawing six feet water.

The south bay contains a number of small islands of salt marsh, which are not susceptible of cultivation, and are only valuable for the grass they produce.

The south side of the town is indented by 10 or 12 small streams or creeks, the greater number of which reach only a small distance above the salt and sedge meadows—they generally take their rise in the swamps, in the woods north of the meadows, and are from 1 to 2 or 3 miles in length. The stream on the west side of Sunquam's Neck,[7] rises in a swamp near the Half Way Hollow Hills, and is 6 or 7 miles in length; none of these streams are navigable above the meadows, but several of them furnish water for mills; and the one on the west of Sunquam's supports 3 grist mills and 4 saw mills. There are also Indian shell banks on several of these creeks.

NATURE OF THE EARTH.

The whole town is evidently alluvial; some have supposed that the elevated land near the sound was not alluvial, but recent discoveries of parts of trees above an hundred feet below the surface in this tract of country, prove that no part of it is of primitive formation.* In no part of the town can the earth be perforated many feet without coming to sand; on the high land, as well as elsewhere a few feet from the surface, you invariably discover the same composition of earth; the usual strata are loam—loam mixed with gravel or sand, and sand with occasional thin strata of loam or marl on the hills, but very seldom elsewhere; and the deeper you go the purer the sand.

On a slope at the west end of the ridge, called the Half-Way Hollow Hills, there is a small tract of land covered with coarse sand stones of a dark yellow colour, some of which appear to be intermixed with some mineral substance. The earth here has been opened,

* Mr. John Velsor, who lives about two miles south west of Cold Spring Harbour in Oysterbay, in digging a well some years since, at the depth of 110 feet, found a part of a tree about 4 feet in length and several inches in diameter entire, with the usual marks distinct, but which soon decayed on its being exposed to the open air.

and a quantity of the sulphuret of iron discovered in a dark coloured moist earth. At the depth of eighteen feet a quantity of the limbs and outer bark of the pitch pine was found, with the cavities and interstices filled with this mineral substance—but whether the branches and bark of the pine are an original deposition in the alluvial formation of the country, or have by some explosion and rupture been let into the earth, as the composition of some of the stones on the surface would seem to indicate, must be left to conjecture.

TIMBER.

The predominant timber on the north side and on the high lands is oak, hickory and chesnut, and with these is an intermixture of various other kinds—the timber on the plains is pitch pine and shrub oak brush, with spots intermixed with a kind of dwarf white oak. Before the revolutionary war the people of Huntington were very careful of their timber, and cut only such as was old and decayed. During the war the British refugees seized the farms of such of the inhabitants as had retired within the American lines, and cut off all the timber, and it was then supposed had ruined the farms; but within a few years, these farms were covered with a fine growth of young timber. This discovery has changed the mode of managing timber land. The practice now universally adopted is to cut the timber entirely off and to keep the sprouts fenced, and in this way it is supposed the timber on the hills and the high land will replace itself in every thirty years.

The town abounds with the plants, shrubs, and flowers of similar climates, and produces a variety of valuable medicinal plants.

ANIMALS.

When the town was first settled, it abounded with several kinds of wild beasts, and wild fowl, that are no longer to be found here, particularly wolves* and wildcats, wild turkeys, swans, and pelicans: deer were formerly abundant, and they still traverse the pine plain, but as there are no large swamps and thickets within the limits of this town to afford them refuge and shelter, they seldom resort here. There are foxes, and squirrels, rabbits, and various other small animals. Birds are plenty, the most valuable are the growse, the partridge, the quail, the plover, and the woodcock.

The south bay abounds with wild fowl in their season; among which are the wild goose, the brant, the broad bill, the widgeon, the black duck, and the sheldrake. The bay also abounds with fish, many of which are animals of passage as well as the birds, among which are the bass, the sheep's head, the weak fish, and various others. Several species of fish are

* November 10th, 1685, the committee who adjusted the charges against the county, allowed £43 13 for forty-three wolves, young and old killed the year preceding, of which number fifteen were killed in Huntington.

taken in the bays on the north side. Lobsters are taken in the sound, and the bays on both sides of the town abound with eels, and most kinds of shell-fish.

Serpents are not numerous; those most frequently seen are the striped snake, the black snake, the water snake, and the adder; the rattle snake is sometimes seen, but very rarely.

HISTORY OF THE FIRST SETTLEMENT.

A settlement was attempted at Huntington as early as 1640, but was interrupted and broken up by Kieft, the Dutch Governor, in 1642, and the people went to the east end of the island and formed a settlement at Southampton, which was the foundation of that town.

The earliest Indian deed for lands in this town, is the deed to Governor Eaton, for Eaton's Neck, in 1646. The first Indian deed[2] to the original settlers of Huntington, was obtained in 1653, and comprises all the lands between Cold Spring and East Cowharbour, and extending from the Sound to the old Country Road, including Horse Neck, which it seems was not intended to be conveyed by the Indians, and was sold in 1654, to three men living in Oysterbay.

This may be considered the date of the first permanent settlement in the town.

It is to be regretted, that we have no account of the transactions or state of the settlement during the first five years from its commencement. The records of those years have by some means or other been destroyed, and all the events connected with that interesting period are unknown.

In 1656, the people of Huntington obtained a deed for the land extending from Cowharbour to Nissaquage River, and from the Sound to the Country Road. Six of the South Necks were purchased in 1657, and three in 1658; the other Neck with the lands lying south of the Country Road, were purchased at different times after that date.

INDIAN PROPRIETORS.

The lands in the town of Huntington[3] were claimed by three different tribes of Indians; the Matinecoes, the Massapeags, and the Secataugs. The first claimed the country from Cold Spring to Nissaquage River, and from the Sound to the old Country Road; the second claimed that part of the town which lies between the old Country Road and the South Bay, as far east as a line from the middle of Copiague north to the said Country Road; and, the third claimed all the remainder of the town.

Wyandance Sachem, of Montauk, in 1659, sold the lands on both sides of the Nissaquage River, extending west as far as Cowharbour, to Lyon Gardiner, of East Hampton, who, in 1663, sold to Richard Smith. Mr. Smith[8] obtained a deed of confirmation for the same lands of the Sachem of the Nissaquage Indians, in 1665, who was dissatisfied with the sale made by Wyandance, and thus became the sole proprietor of Smithfield, as it was then called.

Both these Sachems denied the right of the Matinecoc Indians[4] to the lands between Cowharbour and Nissaquage River, which they had sold to the people of Huntington. [5] The conflicting claims of these different tribes of Indians, produced a long controversy between the people of Huntington and the proprietor of Smithtown, which, after an arbitration and several law suits, terminated in 1675, in a division of the disputed premises between the parties, and the boundary between the two towns was determined to be a line, running from Fresh Pond to Whitman's Hollow; the northwest corner of Winnacomac patent.[9]

STATE OF THE INDIANS.

There is no record of the number of Indians belonging to these tribes, it is presumed, however, that they were considerably numerous. The shell banks around the harbours on the north side, and the creeks on the south side of the town, from their size and number indicate that the population was once very considerable, or must have been stationary there a long time.

Their numbers were such as rendered it prudent for the first settlers to take measures to guard against surprise, and to be prepared to resist any attack that they might make on them.

By a vote of town meeting in 1658, every man was required to be provided with a good gun and sword, and with a certain quantity of powder and lead, and was obliged to assemble, when warned, under a penalty for neglect in any of these respects. The first settlers also erected a fort for their security, which by a vote of town meeting in 1680, they gave to Mr. Jones, their minister, for fire wood. These precautions were probably taken as well against the Indians as the Dutch.

The Duke's laws in 1665, prohibited the sale of arms and ammunition to the Indians, and in 1670, the whites were forbidden to sell horses to them. October 7th, 1681, four Indians came to a store at Cold Spring in the night, and forcibly took two guns and a quantity of rum, tobacco, and venison, and threatened the lives of the family. The first settlers were in the practice of guarding their cattle which they turned in the wood, and it might have been to protect them against the Indians as well as wild beasts, and it is probable they might have been sometimes troublesome to individuals; but the records furnish us no evidence that the settlement was ever interrupted by any general attack by them.

The Indians raised corn and vegetables, and these with the deer, wild fowl, and various kinds of shell fish, and other fish that abounded here, must have afforded them easy and ample means of subsistence. Notwithstanding these advantages, they still continued in the hunter state, and had made no advances in the arts which are usually first cultivated in the infancy of society; they were not distinguished by their dwellings, their clothing, their domestic utensils, or their weapons from the natives of the interior. The only materials of art among them seem to have been some rude vessels of earth hardened in the fire, and these are sometimes found in their shell banks.

They had certain festivals in which it was supposed they worshiped evil spirits, and by the Duke's laws of 1665, it was enacted that " no Indians should at any time be suffered to pawaw, or perform worship to the devil, in any town within the government; " but nothing is now certainly known of the manners, customs or religious sentiments of these tribes of Indians.

At the first settlement of this town, these tribes seem to have been under the influence of Wyandance Sachem, of Montauk, and in some kind of subjection to him. The first purchaser of these tribes deemed it an object to have their deeds signed by him as well as by the Sachem of the tribe who claimed the land. Several of the earliest deeds in this town are executed in this manner. In one of these deeds he is called the Sachem of Paumanacke or Long-Island.

When the first settlements on the island were made, the Indians were at war with the Narraganset Indians who obtained a victory over them, and took the daughter of Wyandance, the Montauk Sachem, captive, who was redeemed by the assistance of Lyon Gardiner, of Gardiner's Island; in gratitude for which, the chief afterwards presented him with a deed for the territory which now forms the town of Smithtown.

By a tradition of the Indians in some parts of the Island, they had been greatly diminished by a raging pestilence a few years before the arrival of the whites among them. They had also been reduced by a war with the Peguods of Connecticut, by whom they were subdued and subjected to tribute. All these tribes have long since disappeared, and not a solitary Indian remains in this town to remind us of the original in-habitants of the country; nor are there any monuments to shew that the country was ever before inhabited, except the shell banks before-mentioned.

STATE OF THE COUNTRY.

The Indians here, as well as every where else where they were settled, annually burnt over the woods in order to clear the land, and to provide food for the deer and other game.

There are numerous facts to prove that at the time of the first settlement of this town, the woods were destitute of under brush, and that the large trees were so scarce, that it was deemed necessary to preserve them from waste, and to prescribe means for their preservation.

The first settlers commenced their improvements immediately without any previous clearing: they enclosed large tracts of land by a common fence for planting, and also for pasturing such part of their stock as they did not wish to run at large.

By a vote of town meeting, 27th December, 1659, they resolved, that if the two half mile squares which had been set apart for planting could not be fenced by the two ends of the town, as was expected, then such as could agree together might look out for a tract fit for corn elsewhere, and fence and improve it in the best way they could.

By a vote, 14th April, 1668, it was concluded to enclose the town plat for common use, for certain portions of their stock which they choose to keep from ranging at a distance, and every man was enjoined to make as much of the fence as was proportionable to the interest which he was to have in the field, in a given time, under the penalty of five shillings for every rod that was not made by that time.

The settlers at first only took up the open land, and suffered the timbered land to remain in common, and subject to the regulations of the town.

In March, 1659, the inhabitants by a vote at town-meeting, resolved that no timber should be cut for sale within three miles of the settlement, under the penalty of five shillings for every tree. In 1660, they made an exception of white oak timber, for pipe staves; but in December, 1668, the constable and magistrates, after stating their apprehensions that the town was in danger of being ruined by the destruction of its timber, ordered, that no timber should be cut or wrought for pipe staves, hogshead staves, or barrel heads, for transportation, on the town commons, within three miles of the settlement, under the penalty of five shillings for every tree so cut, or wrought, contrary to the order; and also forbid the inhabitants to suffer any stranger to cut any timber within the limits of the town, under the like penalty.

The timber in the woods was so thin and sparse, that they abounded with feed, and the people depended on them for pasture for the cattle that were not needed for domestic purposes.

The 30th May, 1665, it was ordered by a vote of town-meeting, that all the young and dry cattle should be driven to Horse Neck to pasture, after the second day of June ensuing.

The 14th April, 1667, by a like vote, it was or-dered, that all the dry and young cattle belonging to the town, should be driven to Crab-Meadow, or be-yond, to Sunken - Meadow, to pasture, the first of May.

It is evident, also, that the Pine plains were bare of brush at this time.

The 7th December, 1663, the inhabitants, at town-meeting, after complaining that great damage was done to the South-Meadows by the swine that found their way there from the settlement, Resolved, that the owners should forthwith fetch them away, and keep them from returning, under a penalty of ten shillings for every one that was suffered to remain there two days, after notice of their being there. It is not probable that the swine would have ranged as far as the south side, if the plains had been covered with brush, as they now are.

By neglecting the Indian practice of annual burnings, in a few years the young timber and underbrush increased so as to injure the feed in the woods.

In 1667, the town Court appointed two men to warn the inhabitants to meet, to fire the woods at such time as they should think fit, and ordered, that every one so warned, should attend, under the penalty of four shillings for every day's neglect.—1st July, 1668, it was voted by the town-meeting, that every male over sixteen years of age, should assemble, when warned by the men who were appointed for that purpose, to cut down brush or underwood when it should be thought a fit time to destroy it, under the penalty of five shillings a day for neglect.

The 7th October, 1672, the governor, by an order, after stating that the feed for horses and cattle in the woods on Long-Island, had decayed by the increase of brush and underwood; directed the inhabitants from sixteen to sixty, to turn out four days in every year, under the direction of the town officers, to cut out the brush and underwood, under the penalty of five shillings for every day's neglect.

MODE OF OBTAINING LAND.

The first settlers purchased their lands of the natives who claimed them; the consideration given for them, was very inconsiderable, and usually consisted of blankets, clothing, fishing implements, and sometimes of guns and ammunition; but, in all cases was such as they deemed an equivalent, and with which they were satisfied. The settlers at first only took up a house-lot

24

in the village, and this is supposed to be all the land taken up, before the first Patent.

Immediately after the conquest of New-York, in 1664, the English governor ordered that the purchasers of Indian lands, should take out letters patent for the confirmation of the purchases, and forbid any further purchases to be made of the natives without a license from the government.

In 1666, the inhabitants of Huntington obtained a patent, by which the whole territory between Cold Spring and Nissaquage river, and between the Sound and the Sea was erected into a Town, with town privileges: the purchases made of the Indians by the inhabitants were confirmed, but the patent gave no power to the inhabitants to purchase the lands which were still held by the Indians within the limits of the Town.

INTEREST OF PROPRIETORS.

The expense of the patent was defrayed by a voluntary contribution of all the inhabitants, and the interest of each in the vacant land was determined to be in proportion to his contribution—a given sum constituted one right, the half of that sum half a right, and double the said sum two rights, and there were as many rights as the said sum was contained in the amount that was paid for the patent—the rights were called hundreds or hundred pound rights.

It is not now known how many rights were under the first patent, nor what was the expense of obtain-

25

ing it. In 1671, there were 90 rights in the whole Town, in 1688, they were reduced to 34, and in 1689 to 70.

It is probable that this reduction took place by the removal of some of the proprietors to other places, and that on such removal they abandoned their rights to the lands not taken up, or that their rights in the same were deemed to be forfeited, and to devolve on those who remained in the Town.

In 1688, the people of Huntington obtained another patent, bounded in the same manner as the former one, which after confirming their titles to the lands which had already been purchased, granted all the remainder of the lands within the limits of the patent, (except the necks on the south side, and the land to the north of them,) absolutely to the inhabitants according to their rights or shares in the original purchases, and also incorporated the Town. The expense of this patent was levied on the proprietors according to their rights in the first patent, and their interests under this patent remained the same as before.

In 1694, they took out their present patent, by which the eastern limit of the Town was altered, their former purchases confirmed, and the right of pre-emption to all the lands within the limits of the patent not then purchased of the Indians was secured to them, and the incorporation of the Town was renewed.

The expense of this patent amounted to £56.18.3, of which sum £50 was paid to the governor and public officers; the whole sum raised was £63.14.10, which was raised by a voluntary contribution of all the inhabitants, and all who contributed became interested in the lands that were not then taken up or appropriated; in proportion to their respective contributions—a right was estimated at 7s. 9d., which made 164 1-2 rights or hundreds in the whole Town.

DIVISION OF THE LANDS.

A division of the land was made among the proprietors when a majority of them agreed to it—previous to every division, they determined what number of acres should be allotted to a right. Two surveyors were annually chosen to make the division, who laid out the land to the several proprietors according to their allotments, and new divisions were made from time to time, until all the lands of any value were taken up.

The number of rights have been reduced under the present patent in the same manner as under the first. In 1731, they were reduced to 137, and probably do not now amount to 100.

In a few instances the proprietors gave certain tracts of land to such persons as were willing to purchase them of the natives; this appears to have been the case with regard to the Baiting place and [10] Square-pit purchases, and also with regard to the purchases of the upland of some or all the necks on the south side.

In two cases, that of the Half-way hollow hill, and of the Yorkers purchase, they sold their right of pre-emption to the purchasers.

OF TRADE.

For some time after the first settlement of the town, the surplus produce of the settlers, as is the case in all new settlements, was needed by the new comers—during this period they had little or no trade, but among themselves, and money was very scarce; contracts were made in produce, and business was carried on by barter and exchanges—contracts for the sale of land, as well as others, were made payable in produce.

In the draft or copy of a contract, between the town and a schoolmaster, dated in 1657, for three years, at the rate of £25 for the first year, £35 for the second, and £40 for the third; the salary is stipulated to be paid in produce, at fixed prices.

In 1686, the town contracted with a carpenter to make an addition to the meeting-house, to be paid in produce, at certain rates.

In 1674, the town erected a mill at Cowharbour, and it is presumed, from circumstances, that the wages of the carpenter were also paid in produce.

In 1682, a farm was sold for £90, payable in nine annual instalments, in produce, at stipulated prices.

Debts were discharged, executions satisfied, and rates paid with produce—the rate at which produce was taken in payment of debts, was the price which the merchants gave for the like articles at the time—produce was taken on execution, on judgments of the town Court, by the same rule, when left to the discretion of the constable.

The Court sometimes designated the articles by which the judgment should be satisfied, and also fixed the prices at which they should be taken.

5th March, 1665, the Court gave judgment that the defendant should pay the debt in wheat, or peas, at merchant's prices, viz: wheat at 4*s*. 6*d*. per bushel, and peas at 3*s*. 6*d*. per bushel;—in these cases, it is conjectured that the Court only enforced the contract of the parties.

Sometimes the Court ordered the debt to be paid in produce, at the current price.

28th January, 1679, the Court gave judgment that the defendant should pay the debt " in good merchantable pay, at the current price."

But generally the Court merely gave judgment for the debt, and left it to the constable to collect it, according to the usage at the time, which was in salable articles, at their current price.

22d September, 1680, the Court gave judgment for the debt, and the constable sold a house and lot, being what had then been allotted to two rights, on execution, at public auction, for £10 10*s*., " to be paid in merchantable pay, at market prices."

Executions issuing out of the Court of Sessions were also levied in produce, but it was appraised by indifferent men, chosen by the parties, or appointed by the sheriff, when it was delivered to the plaintiff in satisfaction of his judgment.

The prices of produce receivable for county rates,

were fixed by the governor and the Court of Sessions, and by the Court communicated to the several towns in the county.

PRICES OF PRODUCE.

In 1665, the assessors were ordered by law, to estimate stock at the following rates:

A horse or mare 4 years old, and upwards,	£12	00	0
Do. between 3 and 4 - - - -	8	00	0
Do. do 2 and 3 - - - -	4	00	0
Do. do 1 and 2 - - - -	3	00	0
An ox or bull 4 years old and upwards, -	6	00	0
A cow, 4 years old and upwards, - -	5	00	0
A steer or heifer between 3 and 4 - - -	4	00	0
Do. do 2 and 3 - -	2	10	0
Do. do 1 and 2 - - -	1	10	0
A goat, 1 year old, - - - - -	0	8	0
A sheep, Do. - - - - - -	0	6	8
A swine, Do. - - - - -	1	00	0

In 1679, the prices fixed by the governor, at which produce should be received for county rates, were as follows:

Pork, - - - -	£0	0	3	per lb.
Beef, - - - - -	0	0	2	Do.
Winter wheat, - -	0	4	0	per bushel.
Summer wheat, - -	0	3	6	Do.
Rye, - - - -	0	2	6	Do.
Indian corn, - - -	0	2	3	Do.
Oil, - - - -	1	10	0	per barrel.

In 1637, the prices of produce receivable for taxes were, as follows:

30

Pork,	-	-	-	-	£3 10 0	per barrel.
Beef,	-	-	-	-	2 00 0	Do.
Wheat,	-	-	-		0 5 0	per bushel.
Indian corn,	-	-	-		0 2 6	Do.
Tallow,	-	-	-		0 00 6	per lb.
Dry hides,	-	-	-		0 00 4	Do.
Green hides,	-	-			0 00 2	Do.

Contract prices of various articles, from 1665 to 1687.

Pork,	-	£3 10 0	per barrel,	or 3*d*. per lb.
Beef,	-	- 1 10 0	Do.	or 2*d*. do.
Butter,	-	0 00 6	per lb.	
Tallow,	-	0 00 6	Do.	
Hog's fat,		0 00 6	Do.	
Wheat, from	0	4 0	per bushel, to 5*s*.	
Rye,	-	0 3 6	Do.	
Corn,	- -	0 2 6	Do.	
Oats,	-	0 2 0	Do.	
Board,	-	0 5 0	per week.	
Victuals,		0 0 6	per meal.	
Lodging,	-	0 0 2	per night.	
Beer,	-	0 0 2	per mug.	
Pasture,	-	0 1 0	for a day and night.	
Labor,	-	0 2 6	per day.	

OF THE CHARACTER OF THE FIRST SETTLERS.

The first settlers of Huntington came either from the New England colonies, or directly from England, and probably some from the one and some from the other. They were probably English independents, and partook of the spirit and temper which at that time characterized that class of men in England.

They adopted every precaution in their power for

the preservation of good morals and good order in their settlement.

ADMISSION OF SETTLERS.

6th July, 1662, the people by a vote at Town-meeting, appointed a Committee consisting of their minister and six of their most respectable inhabitants, to examine the characters of such as came to settle among them, with power to admit or refuse admission to them, as they judged they would be likely to benefit or injure the society, with a proviso that they should not exclude any " that were honest and well approved of by honest and judicious men," and forbid any inhabitant to sell or let house or land to any one but such as should be approved of by said Committee, under the penalty of £10 to be paid to the Town.

10th February, 1663, by vote of Town-meeting, they ordered a certain house and lot to be seized by an attachment for a breach of the aforesaid order.

19th February, 1663, by a vote of Town-meeting, they forbid any inhabitant to entertain a certain obnoxious individual longer than the space of a week either gratuitously or for pay, under the penalty of 40s for the breach of the order " made (as they state) for the peace of the Town."

2d January, 1682, the Town Court ordered the estate of a certain person who was likely to spend it by his extravagance and intemperance, to be *seized* by attachment, that it might be " secured, preserved, and improved for his livelihood and maintenance, and that the Town might not be damnified."

29th June, 1682, the Town Court ordered that an inhabitant who on complaint was convicted of bringing a bag of meal from Oysterbay to Huntington on the Sabbath, should pay a fine of 20s or make an acknowledgment for the offence, such as the Court would accept.

3d June, 1683, the Court required a written acknowledgment such as they prescribed, of three men who were convicted of having travelled from Huntington to Hempstead on the Sabbath, the preceding winter.

18th October, 1660, they established a house of entertainment, and to insure good order, made the continuance of the keeper to depend on the correctness with which he discharged the trust.

In 1657, it would seem they established a school, to be continued for three years under the same teacher.

MINISTRY.

They had a minister settled among them at a very early period of the settlement, if not from its origin.

William Leveredge was a settled minister in the Town in 1659, and had been there some time before, but how long is not known.

February 10th, 1662, the people by a vote of Town-meeting, appointed two men to purchase a house and land for a parsonage, and by a similar vote the 7th June, following, they granted to Mr. Leveredge the use of all the meadow about Cow-Harbour on both sides of the creek, as long as he should continue the minister of Huntington. They also made a vote to raise his salary for a number of years in succession, but it does not appear what the amount of it was.

Mr. Leveredge continued in Huntington until some time between 1670 and 1673, when he left the Town, but for what cause is not stated.

In April, 1673, the people by a vote at Town-meeting, authorized the magistrates, with certain others named for that purpose, to use their endeavours to procure a minister for the Town.

In January, 1676, by a similar vote, they agreed to give Eliphalet Jones an invitation to continue with them as minister, and at the same Town-meeting voted to give him twenty acres of land where he chose to take it up.

Mr. Jones did not give them a definitive answer until June 10th, 1677, nor until after the question whether they desired his continuance with them as their minister, had at his request, again been put to the people assembled at a public training, and was answered in the affirmative by all but one who were present. In 1684, it appears that the salary of Mr. Jones was £50 a year.

Mr. Jones continued the sole minister of Huntington until June 5th, 1723, when on account of his age and infirmities, Ebenezer Prime was ordained and settled as a colleague with him. Mr. Jones gave the charge to

34

Mr. Prime at his ordination, with which he was so much pleased, that he transcribed it into the records of the church, and this is the only authentic production of Mr. Jones that is known.—There is a paper containing the outlines of a discourse among the Town records which is supposed to be his from the date it bears, but that is the only evidence of it.—Mr. Jones lived some years after this period, but it is not known how long. After the death of Mr. Jones, Mr. Prime continued alone the minister of Huntington until October 30th, 1766, when to lighten his labours John Close was ordained and settled as a colleague with him. Mr. Close continued in that capacity until the fall of 1773, when he obtained his discharge and left the town, for what cause does not appear from the records. Mr. Prime after this continued without a colleague until his death in September, 1779—his salary was £70 per year, and his fire-wood.

In 1672, the people contracted with the drummer of the military company, to beat the drum on the Sabbath, to give notice of the time to assemble for public worship; and this practice probably continued till they procured a bell, for which he received ten shillings a year from the Town.

There were forty-three members belonging to the Church at Huntington in 1723, when Mr. Prime was ordained, and the number was very considerably increased during his time.

The constitution of the Church at Huntington was

originally congregational, as was that of all the Churches in the country. In 1748, the people of Huntington were prevailed on to exchange the congregational form of government for that of the Presbyterian, which had been recommended by some of the ministers, and had been adopted through their influence the year before, by several of the congregations in the eastern part of the country.

MEETING-HOUSE.

The first meeting-house in Huntington was built in 1665, an addition of fifteen feet was made to it in 1686. The second meeting-house was built in 1715—it was raised near where the first was erected, but in order to compromise a difference between the inhabitants of the east and west parts of the Town, relative to the proper position of the house, it was taken down and erected on the hill east of the valley where the old one stood. This house continued till the revolutionary war. The British troops stationed in Huntington during the winter of 1777, took possession of it—carried the bell aboard one of their ships, which was afterwards returned so much injured, that it was necessary to have it cast anew—surrounded the house with an intrenchment—tore up the seats and made a storehouse of it. It remained in this condition until the fall of 1782, when it was torn down by order of Colonel Thompson, who commanded the troops then stationed in the Town, and the materials were employed in erecting the barracks in the fort on the burying hill.

An Episcopal Church was erected in Huntington between the years 1750 and 1760. Mr. James Greaton is the only minister that was ever settled in that church. He came to Huntington in the fall of 1767, and continued till his death in the year 1773, after which the church was occasionally supplied by other ministers. A Presbyterian meeting-house was erected between Crab Meadow and Fresh Pond, in the eastern part of the town shortly before the revolutionary war, and was supplied a part of the time by Mr. Hart, the minister of Smithtown.

MILLS.

The first grist mill in Huntington was built in 1660, on the stream running into the harbour, by Mr. Leveredge, the first minister of the town.

A mill was erected by the town on the small stream at Cowharbour in 1674, which was sold to Jeremiah Smith in 1677, on certain conditions, one of which was, that he should not exact more than one quart in sixteen for toll for grinding wheat, nor more than one in twelve for grinding Indian corn.

The privilege of erecting a mill on the stream at Cold Spring, was granted to John Adams, April 1st, 1682. The grant for a mill on Huntington harbour was made to Zophar Patt,[11] April 10th, 1752; and the grant for a mill on Cowharbour was made to Sylvanus Townsend, January 14th, 1774.

It is a condition in all these grants for mills, that the

37

grantees, their heirs, or assigns, shall grind for the people of the town for a fixed toll.

In 1686, the town surveyors were directed to lay out all the ponds or places of water conveniently situated for that purpose, for public watering places.

OF THE POLITICAL STATE OF THE TOWN AT DIFFERENT PERIODS.

Long-Island was claimed both by the English and the Dutch; Kings and Queen's counties were settled under the Dutch; Suffolk county was settled under the English, and in defiance of the Dutch claim.

The several towns in Suffolk county were settled by emigrants from England, and the eastern colonies without any concert with each other—they were not united by any political bond of union, but each was independent of the other, nor were they under the protection or government of any colony.

In this situation, being too remote from the mother country to derive any aid from there, and without connections here, the whole powers of government devolved on the inhabitants of each town. Self-preservation rendered it absolutely necessary that they should assume the exercise of these powers, until a change in their situation should supersede the necessity of their exercise.

AT FIRST A PURE DEMOCRACY.

Thus, each town from its first settlement to the conquest of New York in 1664, was a pure democracy.

The people in each exercised the sovereign power; all questions were determined by the vote of the major-part of the people assembled in town meeting. In this manner they formed such laws and regulations as they judged necessary for the security, peace, and prosperity of their infant settlements.

The town of Huntington was a frontier settlement, and was regarded by the Dutch as an encroachment on their territory. The colonists took sides with their mother countries in the disputes relative to their respective claims to the Island.

MEASURES FOR PUBLIC SECURITY.

The people of Huntington were obliged to take measures for their own security. In order to maintain their settlement from which they had formerly been forced to remove, they took the precaution of providing arms, and erecting a fort as before-mentioned, both against the attacks of the Dutch and the Indians.

The Dutch to check the encroachment of the English, erected a fort in Oysterbay.

These two towns continued to be the limits of the respective claimants until the whole fell under the jurisdiction of the English in 1664.

The people of Huntington at the same time contrived measures for the preservation of internal order as well as external security.

ADMINISTRATION OF JUSTICE.

To secure the administration of justice, and to prevent and punish crimes, they instituted a court which was called the town court, composed of three magistrates, a constable, and clerk, to be chosen annually at town meeting. They invested this court with power to hear and determine all causes civil and criminal. The parties were entitled to a jury if either of them requested it: the jury consisted of seven men, and the verdict was decided by a majority.

It seems that the parties rarely resorted to a jury, as by far the greatest number of decisions are made by the court without a jury.

The judgments of this court extend from a few shillings to fifty pounds and upwards, and affected lands as well as goods and chattels.

In cases of slander, the judgments, when in favor of the plaintiff, are generally in the alternative, that the defendant make verbal satisfaction to the plaintiff in open court, or pay him a certain sum of money. In one case for gross slander and abuse, they adjudged the defendant to the stocks, which is the only instance of corporal punishment mentioned in the records of the court.

It is a remarkable fact and a decisive proof of the purity of the morals of the people, that from the first settlement of the town to the year 1664, it does not appear that a single criminal case came before the court; slander and trespass are the most aggravated offence contained in the records. The proceedings of the court were governed by the principles of the common law, and the acts of the town-meeting.

The decisions of the court were conclusive, and it is to the honour of the magistrates who presided in it, that notwithstanding the extent of their powers, they seem to have exercised them with great fidelity, prudence, and moderation.

The officers of this court frequently made orders relative to matters which concerned the welfare of the town; which seem to have had the same force and effect as the resolutions of the town meeting, from which it is presumed that they were invested with power for this purpose by the voice of the people.

The amount of taxes to be raised for public purposes, was fixed by a vote of the town-meeting; and the rates were made and gathered by persons chosen for that purpose.

Under the benign influence of the common law, and of regulations made by themselves at town meeting, and enforced by a court thus constituted, the people seem to have enjoyed the usual benefit of good government, and to have prospered as well as those settlements that were under the protection of an organized government.

The danger to which the people of Huntington were exposed by their situation, induced them to seek for protection in a connection with some organized colony.

NEGOTIATIONS WITH CONNECTICUT.

In 1658, they choose two men to visit New-Haven for this purpose, but it does not appear that they effected their object.

In 1660, they voted to put themselves under the jurisdiction of Connecticut. In 1662, they choose two deputies to attend the next general court of election, to be held at Hartford, in May, 1663, and as a similar application was made by the eastern towns about the same time, it is probable that they all agreed to become a part of the colony of Connecticut, and subject to its government.

A clause in the charter of Connecticut annexing the islands adjacent to it, to that colony, afforded a pretext for their claiming Long-Island. Accordingly the assembly at Hartford, May 12th, 1664, formally resolved, that Long-Island belonged to the jurisdiction of Connecticut by the terms of the charter, and appointed the governor and two others to go to the island to settle the English plantations there, under the government of Connecticut; to establish quarter-courts, and other courts for the administration of justice, provided their judgments should not extend to life, limb, or banishment, and directed capital cases to be tried at Fairfield, or Hartford.

These commissioners met at Setauket in the summer of 1664, made some decisions on disputed claims, and took some steps towards the objects of their appointment; but these arrangements were all frustrated before they could be carried into effect, by the conquest of the Dutch settlements by the English shortly after they were made.

Long-Island was comprised in the territory which had been conveyed by King Charles the second, to his brother James, the Duke of York, the 12th March, 1664, and he would not suffer any section of country to be detached from it, by any agreement between the inhabitants and any other colony.

THE CONQUEST OF NEW-YORK.

In September, 1664, New-York, then called New-Amsterdam, was taken by the British, and the town of Huntington and the county of Suffolk, were incorporated with the province of New-York, and became subject to the government of the Duke of York.

The people of the several towns in Suffolk county, rejoiced at the conquest, and anticipated great benefits from an organized British government; they flattered themselves that they should be admitted to the common privilege of British subjects, of participating in the formation of the laws, by which they were to be governed; but it was not long before they discovered that they had been too sanguine in their expectations.

Richard Nicoll, the deputy governor under the Duke of York, shortly after he took possession of New-York, convened a meeting at Hempstead, composed of two deputies from every town on the island, for the purpose of adjusting disputed boundaries, and settling the limits of the several towns.

THE DUKE'S GOVERNMENT. [12]

At this meeting the governor promulgated a code of laws which he caused to be framed for the government of the province; which, with the alterations and additions made to them from time to time, continued to be the laws of the province, until October 1683, when the first colony legislature met, and the people were admitted to a share in the legislative power.

These laws which are called the Duke's laws authorize the several towns to elect a constable and eight overseers, who were the assessors of the town, and with the constable were empowered to make regulations respecting matters that concerned the welfare of the town.

The courts established by these laws, were the town-court, the court of sessions, and the court of assize.

The town-court was composed of the constable and two overseers, and had cognizance of all causes under five pounds; the justice of the peace was authorized but not required to preside in this court.

The court of sessions was composed of the justices of the peace of the county, each of whom was allowed £20 a year, and had jurisdiction of all criminal causes, and of civil causes over £5. The judgments of this court for sums under £20 were final; but from such that were for more than that sum, the parties might appeal to the court of assize. Causes were tried in this court by a jury of seven men, in civil cases, and in criminal cases not capital, and the verdict was determined by the voice of the majority; but in capital cases the jury consisted of twelve men, and they were required to be unanimous.

The court of assize was composed of the governor, and such magistrates as he chose to call to his assistance by warrant; suits for demands exceeding £20 might be commenced in this court; so that it had original as well as appellate jurisdiction, and was a court of equity as well as common law.

TYRANNY OF THE DUKE'S GOVERNMENT.

The Duke's laws made no provision for a general assembly, nor did they give the people any voice in the government. The governor possessed unlimited powers, he was commander-in-chief; all public officers were appointed by him, and held their offices during his pleasure; he retained the exclusive power of legislation; could make what laws he pleased, and alter or repeal them when he pleased; he presided in the court of assize, which by appeal had the control of all inferior tribunals. The judgments and decrees of this court were in fact those of the governor; his assistants not being colleagues, but merely advisers.

In this court the governor united the character of both legislator and judge; he not only pronounced what the law was, but prescribed what it should be. All laws subsequent to the code first promulgated are stated in the preface to be made at the court of assize; and many of them were partial and arbitrary, as will always be the case where the people have no voice in legislation.

By an act made at this court, October 8th, 1670, a levy or contribution was ordered to be made in the several towns on the island, to repair the fort at New-York. This the people of Huntington refused to obey, and assigned this among other reasons for their refusal: "because they were deprived of the liberties of Englishmen;" intimating that they deemed it a violation of their constitutional rights, that their money should be taken from them without their consent.

Charles the second, to extend his territories in America by emigration, had declared by proclamation, that the purchases fairly made of the natives should be a valid title. The towns of South-Hampton, South-Old, and Oysterbay, relying on the force of this proclamation, declined taking out patents for the confirmation of their purchases of the Indians in compliance with the governor's order of 1665, which had a retrospective operation in this respect.

By an act made at the court of assize, October 8th, 1670, the titles to land in these towns were declared to be invalid unless patents were taken out for their confirmation within the time specified in the act.

By a proclamation of governor Andross, 26th November, 1674, a term of the court of sessions, in Suffolk county, was suspended, and the towns of Setauket, and Huntington, were ordered to have their business for that term transacted at the ensuing court of sessions at Jamaica, in Queen's county; because the towns of East-Hampton, South-Hampton, and South-Old, had not returned the accounts of the constables and overseers of those towns to the governor according to his orders.

April, 1682, the people of Huntington, at town-meeting, voted to make provision for the time and expenses of five of their citizens "who were forced to New-York, and suffered imprisonment" under the same governor, on what pretence is not stated; but as a meeting of delegates from the several towns was held there shortly before, for the purpose of deliberating on their political condition, it is conjectured that it was to punish them for daring to exercise the rights of freemen.

FIRST LEGISLATURE.

The arbitrary measures of the Duke's governors produced so much discontent, that he was at length compelled to admit the people to a share in the legislative power. The first general assembly met in October 1683, after which the Duke's laws ceased to operate, except such as were adopted or recognized by the legislature.

The innovations made on the Duke's laws for the administration of justice by the legislature of 1683, are contained in the act published in the appendix to the second volume of the revised laws of 1813.

ARBITRARY POWER OF THE GOVERNOR.

After the organization of the colony legislature, the governor still retained many prerogatives which he exercised in an arbitrary manner: he had the whole power over the public lands: no purchase could be made without his licence, and no purchase was of any avail unless confirmed by patent within a limited time, and for these he extorted such sums from the applicants as his avarice dictated.

The fees of patents constituted the principal perquisites of the governor, and the quit rent charged on them formed no inconsiderable part of the public revenue.

The interest which the governors had in these, operated as an inducement to multiply the number of patents and enlarge the quit rents as much as possible.

In 1685, governor Dongan issued a patent to certain persons who did not reside in the town, for the lands which had been in dispute between the people of Huntington and the proprietor of Smith-Town, and had been divided between them by the Court of Assize in 1675, which created a law-suit, but was never carried into effect. In 1686, the governor ordered the people of Huntington to purchase the lands within their patent which were not then purchased of the Indians, in order that they might be compelled to take out a new patent.

The quit rent charged on the patent of Huntington was not fixed, and the amount which that should be was a source of perpetual altercation between the people of Huntington and the Duke's governors. To compel them to consent to its being fixed agreeable to his wishes in 1686 or 1687, Governor Dongan seized their patent, and before he would consent to grant a confirmation of it, they were obliged to agree to raise £29 4 7 in satisfaction of their quit rent, and for the expense of a new patent, which was granted in 1688, and the quit rent fixed at 20 shillings a year.

APPLICATION TO CONNECTICUT.

These and the like arbitrary proceedings of the governors induced the people of Huntington to unite with the people of the other towns in the county, in an unsuccessful effort to connect themselves with the colony of Connecticut, the laws and institutions of which were more congenial with their ideas of good government than those of the Duke of York, who had now become King James the Second.

OF THE REVOLUTION IN FAVOUR OF WILLIAM AND MARY.

The abuses which they had suffered under the governors, prompted the measures that were taken in New-York in 1689, in favour of the great revolution, then going on in England, in behalf of William and Mary, and which terminated in the expulsion of James the Second from the throne, and forever put an end to his authority.

The patent of 1688 was signed just at the commencement of those divisions respecting the measures taken in favour of the revolution in England which distracted the colony for several years, and was not carried into effect before the government was quietly settled under the new order of things, when the people of Huntington, in order to fix the limits between them and Smith-Town, agreeable to their respective titles in 1694, took out their present patent in which the quit rent was fixed at 40 shillings a year, and which they discharged by commutation under act of the legislature of this state in 1787.

OF THE ROYAL GOVERNORS.

The royal governors, after the revolution in 1689, in many respects resembled their predecessors; they manifested the same disposition to get what they could from the people, and the same inclination to rule without control, although they had less power to gratify their inclinations. The whole colony administration exhibits a constant conflict between the claims and encroachments of power on the one hand, and the spirit of liberty struggling to defeat them on the other.

OF THE AMERICAN REVOLUTION.

The arbitrary measures of the provincial governors taught the people to investigate and to understand their rights, and prepared them for the revolution that terminated in the independence of the country. The people of Huntington were almost unanimously in favour of it, and they suffered all manner of hardships and privations during the war.

The powers of the colony governor were suspended at the commencement of the revolution, and the government was administered by a provincial congress, aided by town and county committees—Public spirit supplied the place of authority, and gave the recommendations of these bodies the force of law.

The Island was surrendered the 29th of August, 1776, and in October, governor Tryon came to Huntington, called the people together, and by threatening imprisonment and banishment compelled the committee, by a written declaration, to disavow and condemn all their proceedings, and obliged them and the people generally, to take the oath of allegiance. The committees of the other towns and of the county, were compelled in the same manner to sign a similar declaration, and the people to take the same oath.

SUFFERINGS DURING THE WAR.

But this submission afforded them no protection to their persons or property; they were not treated as subjects or prisoners, but according to the caprice of every temporary commander. The whole country within the British lines was subject to martial law. The administration of justice was suspended; the army was a sanctionary for crimes and robbery, and the grossest offences were atoned by enlistment.

The British troops were stationed in Huntington, at different times during the war, and the persons of the inhabitants were subjected to the orders, and their property to the disposal, of the British officers.

They compelled some to enlist—others to stand guard, and obliged the people generally, to do all kinds of personal services; to work at the forts, to go with their teams on foraging parties, and to transport their cannon, ammunition, provisions and baggage from place to place, as they changed their quarters, and to go and come on the order of every petty officer who had the charge of the most trifling business.

In 1781, the town was compelled to raise £176 by a general tax, as a commutation for personal labour towards digging a well in the fort, on Lloyd's Neck. The officers seized and occupied the best rooms in the houses of the inhabitants. They compelled them to furnish blankets and fuel for the soldiers, and hay and grain for their horses. They pressed their horses and wagons for the use of the army; they took away their cattle, sheep, hogs, and poultry, and seized without ceremony and without any compensation, or for such only as they chose to make, for their own use whatever they desired to gratify their wants or wishes.

In the fall of 1782, at the conclusion of the war, about the time the provisional articles of the treaty of peace were signed in Europe, Colonel Thompson, (since said to be Count Rumford,) who commanded the troops then stationed at Huntington, without any assignable purpose, except that of filling his own pockets by its furnishing him with a pretended claim on the British treasury for the expense caused a fort to be erected in Huntington, and without any possible motive except to gratify a malignant disposition by vexing the people of Huntington, he placed it in the centre of the public burying ground, in defiance of a remonstrance of the trustees of the town, against the sacrilege of disturbing the ashes and destroying the monuments of the dead.

In April, 1783, Sir Guy Carleton instituted a board of commissioners for the purpose of adjusting such demands against the British army as had not been settled. The accounts of the people of Huntington for property taken for the use of the army, which were supported by receipts of British officers, or by other authentic vouchers; which were prepared to be laid before the board, amounted to £7249. 9s. 6d. and these accounts were not supposed to comprise one fourth part of the property which was taken from them without compensation.

These accounts were sent to New-York to be laid before the commissioners, but they sailed for England before they had examined them, and the people from whom the property was taken were left (like their neighbours, who had received no receipts for the property taken from them,) without redress.

But the inhabitants of Huntington sustained the greatest abuse from the British refugees; who, when ever they could shelter themselves under any colour of authority, did all the injury in their power; they seized the farms of such of the inhabitants as had gone into the American lines; destroyed the timber, and

53

suffered them to go to ruin. Those among them who had no character or property, generally resorted to Lloyd's Neck, and devoted themselves to pillage and robbery; it was a common practice with them to hang the inhabitants whom they robbed, until they were nearly dead, to compel them to give them their money, and if they were detected, they enlisted, and this arrested the arm of justice, shielded them from punishment, and enabled them to bid defiance to those whom they had robbed and abused.

These abuses evinced the value of that maxim of free states that makes the military subordinate to the civil power, and taught the inestimable value of civil laws and legal liberty.

NOTES.

When this pamphlet was written by its distinguished author, it was to call attention to the advantages presented by that part of Long Island, as a place of permanent residence. Previous to the Revolution, Long Island was the most important portion of the Colony of New York, and it was like a hive that at different intervals sent out swarms of inhabitants to settle in other regions. In fact, the Counties along the Hudson river, had in addition to their original inhabitants, a very large population which originally came from Long Island. Mr. Wood's great desire was not only to check this emigration, but to attract settlers from other parts. The pamphlet which was printed for gratuitous distribution, attracted much attention at the time, and to some extent realized the hopes of its honored author.

The patent granted to the town of Huntington by Governor Richard Nicoll, Nov. 30, 1666, recites: "Whereas there is a certain Town within this Government called and known by the name of Huntington, now in the tenure and occupation of several Freeholders and Inhabitants." The same is "confirmed to Jonas Wood, Wm. Leveridge, Robert Seeley, John Ketcham, Thomas Skidmore, Isaac Platt, Thomas Jones and Thomas Weeks, in behalf of themselves and associates." Their bounds were "From a certain river or creeke on the west commonly called by the Indyans by the name of Nackagnatok, and by the English the Cold Spring, and to stretch eastward to Nasaquack river, on the north to be bounded by the Sound, running betwixt Long Island and the maine, and on ye South by ye Sea, including nine several necks of meadow ground, All which tracts of land together with the said necks, are to belong to the said Town of Huntington."

HORSE NECK. NO. 2 (PAGE 2).

This Neck, called in later years "Lloyd's Neck," was purchased from its original owners by John Richbell. His title was disputed by John Conkling, of Southold, but the title of Richbell was sustained. He sold it to Nathaniel Sylvester, Thomas Hunt and Latimer Sampson and a patent was granted to them by Gov. Nicoll, Nov. 20, 1667, although it was included within the limits of the Patent to Huntington. Nathaniel Sylvester sold his share to the other two owners. Latimer Sampson left his share by will to Grizzell, the eldest daughter of Nathaniel Sylvester, and the share of Thomas Hunt was sold by his attornies, Robert Story and John Brown, to James Lloyd, of Boston. He married Grizzell Sylvester, and thus the whole tract came to them. Gov. Thomas Dongan granted a Patent to James Lloyd, March 18, 1685, and established it as a "Lordship and manor of Queen's village," with full manorial rights. This manorial government continued down to the revolution, nearly 100 years. It was then abolished and the territory was annexed to Queen's County. In recent years it has been restored, and is now a part of Suffolk County.

THE FIRST PURCHASE. NO. 2 (PAGE 16).

The first purchase of lands in Huntington was made from Raskokan, Sagamore of Matinecock, by Richard Houldbrook, Robert Williams and Daniel Whitehead, April 2, 1653, "Bounded on the West side with a river commonly called by the Indians Nackaquetock, on the north by the Sea [Sound], and going eastward to a river called Opcatkantyoke,* and on the south side to the utmost part of my bounds." This deed is signed by 22 Indians.

ORIGIN OF NAME. NO. 3 (PAGE 17).

The original name of the tract embraced in this town was Ketewamoke. The town was called Huntington probably in

---

* This is the stream at the head of Northport Harbor.

honor of the village in England, which was the birthplace of Oliver Cromwell.

THE EASTERN PURCHASE. NO. 4 (PAGE 18).

"On or about the Last day of July, 1656," the Indian Sachem Asharakan sold to Jonas Wood, Wm. Rogers and Thomas Wilkes "All the meadows, fresh and salt, lying and being on the north side of Long Island, from our former bounds, Cow Harbor brooke, to Nessequake river." This was called the Eastern Purchase. All that part that lies east of Unthemamuck, or the Fresh Pond, was claimed by Richard Smith, the founder of Smithtown, on the ground that it was not the property of the above-named Sachem, but was a part of the land conveyed by the Mantauk Sachem, Wyandauch, to Lyon Gardiner. After a long controversy, the claim of Richard Smith was sustained.

THE SOUTH PURCHASE. NO. 5 (PAGE 18).

On June 1, 1667, Wyandouch the Great Sachem of Mantauk, sold to Jonas Wood, "for himself, and the rest of his neighbors of Huntington," "Five necks of meadow lying next adjoining to Massapeags Sachems' lands." This was the first Indian deed for lands on the south side of Long Island in Huntington. These necks were bounded on the north by the "Old Indian Path," which was the ancient fording place where the Indians crossed the heads of the various creeks.

On Aug. 17, 1658, Wyandanch sold to Henry Whitner, of Huntington, "for the use of the whole town of Huntington," "three whole necks of meadow lying on the southward side of that town, and westwardly from the 6 necks which we bought heretofore."

This deed was executed through Cockenoe, the famous Indian interpreter, as agent for Wyandanch. Among the various articles given for this tract was "A Great Fine Looking Glass." This is probably the first mention of a looking glass in Suffolk County.

From these tables it will be seen that in 1820, Huntington was the second town in the county in wealth and population. A few years later the proportion was greatly changed, especially by the sudden growth of villages like Sag Harbor, which is now and has been for some years, the largest village.

BABYLON.

In old times the region now embraced in the town of Babylon was known as "Huntington South." The town of Babylon was established in 1872.

The village of Babylon is situated on a neck known in early times as Sumpwam's Neck. The following article from Dr. Wm. Wallace Tooker, the distinguished student of the Indian language, explains its meaning:

THE NAME SUMPWAMS AND ITS ORIGIN.
NO. 7 (PAGE 12).

BY WM. WALLACE TOOKER.

The name *Sumpwams* appears about twenty-one times in the printed records of the town of Huntington, with the following leading variations in orthography, viz.: *Sampawame, Sumpwams, Sowampams,* 1689; *Sumpawams,* 1690; *Sampaumes,* 1697; *Sumpwams,* 1740; and, although "commonly so-called" in 1689, it does not appear earlier in the records. It is evident from the insistence of the English possessive, that the neck of land on which the name was originally bestowed, derives its appellation from an Indian named *Sampawam* or *Sumpwam,* who formerly lived and planted there. There are other necks of land extending into Great South Bay, and contingent waters, which take their Indian names from like circumstances. I am aware that no Indian, designated by this name in its entirety, can be found mentioned in the records; but there is one, however, whose popular cognomen among the settlers, may be a curtailed reminder of *Sumpwams.* In the "Indian deed for

58

Sumpwams' Neck " (H. R. Vol. i. p. 171), his name is written
" pwamas," which is seemingly near enough to the conclusion,
that this name in its various forms, seldom twice alike, is a collo-
quial contraction. Similar change is noticed in the English contraction *"Siases"* for Josiah's Neck in the same township. The
meaning of *Sumpwams* is the "straight walker" or "he goes
straight," hence, an "upright or just man." The prefix *Sump*
or *Saump*, being the equivalent of the Narragansett *Saumpi;*
Massachusetts *Sampwi*, signifying primarily "straight," "di-
rect," and by metonymy, "just," upright, right in action or
conduct, being used more often in this sense than in the other by
Eliot in his Indian Bible. The terminal is the verb of motion,
in the third person singular — *aum* ⚊ *8m*, or as Eliot sometimes
wrote it, *w8m*, "he goes," hence we have in Eliot's notation
Samp-w8m's Neck.

The full account of the lengthy controversy between Smithtown and Huntington may be found in the printed volume of
Smithtown Records. No. 8 (page 17).

The tract of land known as Winnecomac, now a part of Smithtown, was an independent purchase made by Charles Congreve,
and the greater part of which was afterwards owned by Rip Van
Dam, a very prominent citizen of New York. A dispute between
the owners of the tract, and the town of Huntington, as regards
the south line was settled by agreement. No. 9 (page 18).

"Square Pit purchase" is a misprint for Squaw pit purchase,
a well known tract near the middle of the town. No. 10 (page 27).

Zophar Patt is a misprint for Zophar Platt, a very prominent
member of a well known family. For a full account, see Thompson's Hist. of L. I. No. 11 (page 37).

The Code enacted by the Duke of York was published in a
manuscript volume, copies of which were sent to each town. So
far as we know only two of these original copies are in existence,
one in Huntington, and one in Southampton. The whole was
printed many years since by the New York Historical Society.
No. 12 (page 44).

59

INDEX.

61

www.ingramcontent.com/pod-product-compliance
Lightning Source LLC
Chambersburg PA
CBHW020236090426
42735CB00010B/1723